Find It in Nature!

Animal Tracks

by Jenna Lee Gleisner

Bullfrog Books

Ideas for Parents and Teachers

Bullfrog Books let children practice reading informational text at the earliest reading levels. Repetition, familiar words, and photo labels support early readers.

Before Reading

- Discuss the cover photo. What does it tell them?

- Look at the picture glossary together. Read and discuss the words.

Read the Book

- "Walk" through the book and look at the photos. Let the child ask questions. Point out the photo labels.

- Read the book to the child, or have him or her read independently.

After Reading

- Prompt the child to think more. Ask: Have you ever seen animal tracks? Did you know what animals made them? How could you tell?

Bullfrog Books are published by Jump!
5357 Penn Avenue South
Minneapolis, MN 55419
www.jumplibrary.com

Library of Congress Cataloging-in-Publication Data

Names: Gleisner, Jenna Lee, author.
Title: Animal tracks / by Jenna Lee Gleisner.
Description: Minneapolis: Jump!, Inc., 2024.
Series: Find it in nature! | Includes index.
Audience: Ages 5–8
Identifiers: LCCN 2023019221 (print)
LCCN 2023019222 (ebook)
ISBN 9798889966746 (hardcover)
ISBN 9798889966753 (paperback)
ISBN 9798889966760 (ebook)
Subjects: LCSH: Animal tracks—Juvenile literature.
Classification: LCC QL768 .G58 2024 (print)
LCC QL768 (ebook)
DDC 591.47/9—dc23/eng/20230424
LC record available at https://lccn.loc.gov/2023019221
LC ebook record available at https://lccn.loc.gov/2023019222

Editor: Katie Chanez
Designer: Molly Ballanger

Photo Credits: Shutterstock, cover; Tsekhmister/Shutterstock, 1; Eric Isselee/Shutterstock, 3, 22 (bear), 22 (raccoon), 23tl, 24; vgajic/iStock, 4; Marina Demidiuk/Shutterstock, 5, 23bl; Imgorthand/iStock, 6–7; photomaster/Shutterstock, 8, 22 (turkey); K Steve Cope/Shutterstock, 8–9; leonikonst/iStock, 10–11; Mike Tan/Shutterstock, 11; Michael-Tatman/iStock, 12; txking/iStock, 13; Sonsedska Yuliia/Shutterstock, 14; Ken Kistler/Alamy, 14–15; 5th Gate Photography/Shutterstock, 16–17; Jim Cumming/Shutterstock, 17, 22 (rabbit); Heatherfaye/iStock, 18; RAUL RODRIGUEZ/iStock, 19, 23tr; Kennethawhite88/Dreamstime, 20, 22 (duck), 23br; NataliaSokko/iStock, 20–21; WilleeCole Photography/Shutterstock, 22 (deer); anat chant/Shutterstock, 22 (snake).

Printed in the United States of America at Corporate Graphics in North Mankato, Minnesota.

Table of Contents

Tracking Animals

We are in a forest.

Animals were here!

They left tracks in the mud.

track

5

What animals were here?

Tracks will tell us.

Let's find more!

Look!

A turkey walked here.

A turkey foot has three long toes.

Bear paws are big.
Each has five toes.
They have claws, too!

claw

Deer hooves are shaped like hearts.

hoof ·····▶

hand

foot

15

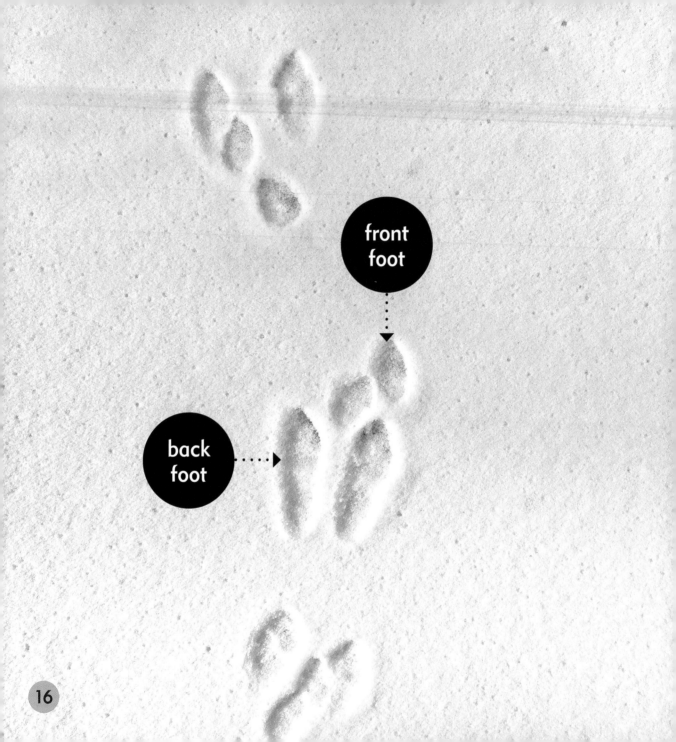

front
foot

back
foot

16

A rabbit hopped here.
Rabbits have long back feet.
Their front feet are small.

Look! A snake track!

It is a wavy line.

Why?

Snakes do not walk.

They slither on their bellies.

Ducks have webbed feet.

They leave tracks
in the sand.

Have you seen
animal tracks?

21

Match the Tracks

Match each animal with its tracks. Look back at the book if you need help!

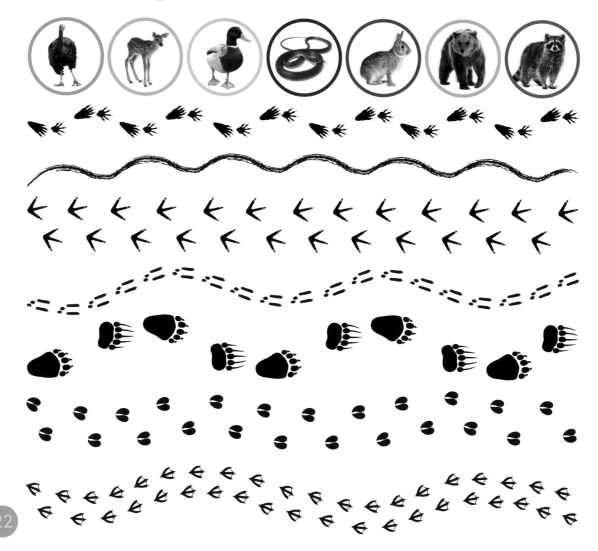

heels
The backs of feet.

slither
To move along by sliding.

tracks
Marks that a moving animal
leaves behind.

webbed
Connected by folds of skin.

Index

To Learn More

Finding more information is as easy as 1, 2, 3.

❶ Go to www.factsurfer.com

❷ Enter "animaltracks" into the search box.

❸ Choose your book to see a list of websites.

FACT SURFER

FIND IT IN NATURE!

What do bear tracks look like? What kind of tree has needles instead of leaves? Learn to identify forest flowers, mushrooms, trees, leaves, and animal tracks in this fun series! Have you read them all?

www.jumplibrary.com
www.jumplibrary.com/teachers

IL: Grades K–3   GRL: E

ISBN 979-8-88996-675-3

90000
9 798889 966753